Teenage Survival Guide

An A-Z guide to getting the Christian life sorted

Eleanor Watkins

kevin
mayhew

kevin
mayhew

First published in Great Britain in 2008 by Kevin Mayhew Ltd
Buxhall, Stowmarket, Suffolk IP14 3BW
Tel: +44 (0) 1449 737978 Fax: +44 (0) 1449 737834
E-mail: info@kevinmayhewltd.com

www.kevinmayhew.com

9 8 7 6 5 4 3 2 1

ISBN 978 1 84867 107 2
Catalogue No. 1501145

Cover design by Rob Mortonson
Edited by Katherine Laidler
Typeset by Dave Cullen

Printed and bound in Great Britain

Introduction

It's not easy being a teenage girl, and today's world is not an easy one to live in. Even during the last ten years there have been changes in the world scene and in our own society that make life harder and grittier, and sometimes growing up in it may seem a scary prospect. Add to that the fact that you are growing and changing, physically, emotionally and spiritually, and it can all feel very daunting. Don't despair. God knew what he was doing when he created you to live here and now in the twenty-first century. It's probably the most exciting and challenging of all times to live, and he has an amazing plan for your life – one that will bring you the maximum happiness and fulfilment. God can be trusted to stick with you at every stage. And he loves to hear the sound of your laughter!

This A-Z comes with the hope that, in its pages, you will find help, reassurance, guidance, answers to your questions and encouragement to press on in your Christian life. Please get in touch if you'd like to – I'd love to hear from you!

Eleanor Watkins

Aa

Acne

Acne is the pits and so are all the other types of spot, blemish, pimple and zit just waiting to erupt from your otherwise clear skin. Have you noticed how a spot won't show itself until the very day you have an important interview or a special party, or there's a fit new guy in the area that you'd really like to make an impression on? It's not a bit of use your mum or your best mate telling you the spot is miniscule and hardly visible without an extra-strong magnifying glass, and that a bit of concealer will completely disguise it. You just know that it's huge, and red, and completely gross and off-putting.

Seriously, acne is common among young people as it's hormone-related. Males suffer more than females. It's worse in people with oily skins, and usually clears up of its own accord by your early 20s.

If you're 14 and spotty, that's not much consolation, but don't despair. Help is available. Severe acne can be controlled by medication from the doctor, but there are some things you can do to help yourself.

- Sunshine is beneficial, although be careful of sunburn and always use suncream when you're out in the sun.

- Wash the affected areas carefully twice a day, using warm water and a mild, pure, non-perfumed soap (for example, Simple soap.)

- Tea tree oil works wonders at clearing up spots.

- Antiseptic cream such as Germolene can help with healing spots that are infected, but see your doctor if they don't begin to heal in a few days.

- Above all, don't pick or squeeze spots – this spreads infection and can leave scars.

AIDS

Whatever your standpoint, AIDS is here and shows no sign of going away. AIDS is a killer with no easy cure as yet. Safe sex is repeatedly promoted as protection, but the only real protection is keeping sex within marriage. This may seem tough, but it's a fact.

Nevertheless, there are myths about AIDS. The HIV virus is only passed on through the sharing of body fluids – in sexual intercourse, contact with infected blood or use of a dirty hypodermic needle. It is not passed on from lavatory seats, clothing, hugging, touching or even kissing.

AIDS is not the judgement of God, who wants the best for his beloved children. It is a tragic result of ignoring the rules God has laid down for our health and happiness.

Alcohol Abuse

A lot of people don't realise that alcohol is actually a powerful drug. Its effects are even stronger on a young person, and girls are more susceptible than boys. Sadly, in today's culture the over-use of alcohol is seen as 'cool'.

Binge-drinking is commonplace and a good night out seems to be measured by the amount of alcohol consumed. This is one of Satan's more blatant lies and part of his plan to destroy the lives of young people. Is it really enjoyable to be so drunk you're off your face, out of control, wake up with a splitting headache, upset stomach and, worst of all, not quite remember what happened the night before? Even if you don't intend to drink much, it's easy to get carried away when others are knocking it back. And be aware that it's all too easy for a drink to be spiked by some idiot who thinks it's a big joke.

Alcohol is absorbed into the bloodstream more quickly on an empty stomach. It has a strong depressant action on the nervous system, slowing down brain activity and affecting co-ordination, judgement and emotions. The short-term effects of alcohol abuse include headaches, nausea, vomiting, dehydration, accidents, aggression and hangovers; inhibitions are lessened and judgement is impaired. Long-term effects can be damage to the liver and heart, brain and nervous systems, depression, personality changes and dependence.

Is it cool to drink to excess? Work it out for yourself and have a read of Romans 6:13.

Animals

Animals are great. A pet is always pleased to see you, usually welcomes a cuddle, listens to all your woes and doesn't answer back. The saddest thing about pets is that their lifespan is short and, sooner or later, they'll grow sick or old and die.

Losing a pet is a true bereavement and takes time to get over. Cry for them as much as you need to, but don't feel guilty. Remember the good times you had together. When you're ready, welcome a new pet into your life and enjoy it.

Taking care of a pet is good discipline. It needs to be fed, exercised, groomed and kept clean. You can't shove it into a cupboard or garage like a bike or a pair of roller-blades when you're tired of it.

A pet is for life.

Anorexia

see Eating Disorders

Arguments

see Families, Rows

Bb

Bedrooms

Your bedroom is likely to be the place where you go to relax, chat online, text, sleep, enjoy privacy, read, study, listen to music, think, let your hair down and generally chill out.

A bedroom is said to reflect the personality of its occupant. I hesitate to guess what yours says about you, because it's quite likely to be a jumble of discarded clothing, wet towels, books, magazines, soft toys, sweet wrappers, bags, shoes and open doors and cupboards! Posters of cuddly animals probably rub shoulders with gorgeous boy bands on the tastefully decorated walls, and the air is heavy with the scent of body spray. You have stuck drawing pins in places where pins ought not to be stuck, and a felt-tipped pen has leaked on to the pale lilac carpet, where you flung it when you were dumped by text by your last-but-one boyfriend in the middle of your homework essay. At the same time, you knocked over a half-full coffee mug, which has left a brown stain that refuses to come out.

Whenever a friend is sleeping over, you have a blitz which leaves your room neat, dusted, vacuumed and free of clutter. The guest has to be careful of just one thing though: she must never, ever, open the cupboard door, or she is in danger of being buried alive under the avalanche of stuff that will burst out!

Best Friends

Everyone needs a best friend, though sometimes they can be a mixed blessing. A while ago your best friend was Abs, who proved traitorous by talking about you behind your back and then going off with your boyfriend. Then there was Sami, who had the habit of ignoring you when anyone more interesting came along (which seemed to be quite often).

At the moment your best mate is Kayleigh and you get along pretty well, apart from the occasional difference of opinion. She does have a bit of an attitude problem, but you and she are quite happy to spend hours talking over the causes and effects of it. In fact, school hours are nowhere near long enough for this, and you have to text one another constantly at home, when you're travelling and anywhere else where you can't actually talk. It always amazes you that the credit on your phone lasts such a short time.

Ideally, a best friend should be loyal, supportive, discreet, generous, slow to take offence and quick to forgive. She should be willing to share, listen, advise, console, pick up pieces, and lend a shoulder to cry on and her funky strappy top for Saturday night. She should never divulge a confidence or repeat a word of any secret entrusted to her ears.

It's not an ideal world, though, and your best friend will probably let you down in at least some of these departments. Don't forget that it's quite possible that you will do the same.

Bible

Young Christians (and indeed all Christians) need regular portions of the Bible to nourish them, just as much as we all need three square meals a day to feed our bodies.

The Bible is a collection of books – history, poetry, teaching and story-telling – written by various authors under the inspiration of God. It tells of God's creation of the world, the history of its peoples, collected writings of its poets and prophets, all pointing to the coming of Jesus Christ, God's Son, about whom the New Testament was written and whose life and death is central to the Christian faith.

Bibles come in many translations and modern versions these days. The King James Authorised version has beautiful language and imagery, but some of the modern forms are easier to understand and relate to life in today's world. Some are paraphrased into modern everyday language, while others may have cartoon-like illustrations. There are also Youth Bibles with specially marked passages of Scripture.

Whichever you choose, a set of study notes is helpful to get you started and help you understand and apply what you are reading to your own life. It's a great idea to memorise Scripture verses, which are then stored away deep inside you for use when you need them. Bible study and discussion groups with other young people can be stimulating, exciting and a real source of discovery, encouragement and growth. (Read 2 Timothy 3:14–4:5.)

Boredom

Life can be boring. At times it's very boring, like when there's nowhere to go, nothing to do and nobody to do it with. It doesn't help when parents make comments like 'If you're bored, you can help me chop onions for the shepherds' pie/scrub the toilets/go and do the shopping for Grandma' or 'I wish I had the time to be bored!'

Most adult conversations are boring as well. So are long car journeys with your parents. So are some books you have to read for your literature course. So are some church services. The list could continue.

Maybe the best antidote to boredom is someone else your own age to be bored with – or maybe just considering someone else besides yourself.

Boys

Boys seem to appear on the scene when you are about 11 or 12. They must have been there before, of course, but you probably only noticed them for their nuisance value.

Suddenly they are everywhere, with long arms and legs and deeper voices, and a habit of looking at you out of the corner of their eye as you walk down the street. They like to hang together with other boys, and do a lot of laughing and thumping each other and looking big.

Boys would like you to believe that they are tough, macho and independent. In fact, they have at least as many hang-ups and insecurities as girls.

It's cool to be on friendly terms with lots of boys, so don't be in too much of a hurry to meet that special one!

Boyfriends *see also Relationships*

It's a great boost to your morale when a boy asks you out. You don't have to accept. Ask yourself some questions first:

- Do you really like him?
- Do you trust him?
- What does he mean by 'going out?'
- What do you mean by 'going out?'

If you're a Christian, you're wise to stick to boys who are Christians too. You may think you'll be able to influence that gorgeous non-Christian, get him converted and live happily ever after. It hardly ever works like that. More likely, you'll find yourself pulled in different directions, which is uncomfortable if not downright painful.

If in doubt, take great care. Ask advice from your best friend by all means, but also from trusted people who are a little older and more experienced. These could be a young couple at your church, or your youth leader, or even (yes, really) your own mum or dad. You'll be surprised how much they might remember from their long-gone youth.

Don't fall into the trap of thinking any boy is better than no boy. On the other hand, you need to get to know as many as possible, so that you recognise a really good one when he comes along.

Bras
see also Clothes, Diets

Bra sizes can create a lot of worry, but there's really no need. Bust sizes vary a great deal and virtually all are normal. People develop at different rates, so don't be tempted to compare yourself with friends.

It's important, though, to get the right-sized bra, one that fits correctly and gives the right support. Wearing your older sister's cast-offs is not a good idea, nor one that is ancient and grey and stretched out. Get fitted by a proper expert, and re-fitted as you grow.

Finally, never feel embarrassed about your developing bustline, whatever its size. Don't develop a round-shouldered stoop to disguise it. Be proud that you're growing into the attractive woman God planned for you to be.

Brothers

On the whole, brothers can be an advantage, especially if they're older than you. Older brothers are useful in many ways. They may even have cool shirts and jackets and other gear for borrowing – as long as they never find out! A girl can have a certain street-cred among her peers if she has an older brother, especially if he's a fit guy.

At best, older brothers will protect you from hassle, plead your case with irate parents or bail you out with a few pounds when you're skint. They may bully you a bit and you will have to tread warily around their girlfriends. It's worth the effort, though, especially if your brother has passed his driving test and has his own set of wheels!

Bullying

see also Verbal Abuse

Bullying is very common indeed, at all ages and stages. Most people are bullied to some degree or other at some time during their school life. Sometimes it's a passing thing, especially if you're a fairly confident person to begin with. Not everyone is, however. Unfortunately, it's the nature of a bully to target someone who stands out or is different or vulnerable in some way, and a lot of further damage can be done to someone who is already insecure, lonely or hurt.

Bullies are almost always unhappy and inadequate people themselves. They need to dominate or ridicule others to boost their own low self-esteem. Usually they depend on their hangers-on to support them. Alone, they become pathetic people.

The only way to deal with a bully is to stand up to him or her. You will almost certainly need help to do this. If you're being bullied, tell someone: a parent or a teacher or some other adult you trust. There may be threats of repercussions, or you may be called a grass, or worse. Take no notice. Teachers usually know the score and how best to deal with it. Suffering in silence is doing no one any favours, the bullied person or the bullies themselves.

Sadly, people who are persistently bullied sometimes react by picking on someone smaller and weaker than themselves. It takes guts to break the cycle, but it can be done!

Cc

Careers
see also Jobs, Work

Some fortunate people know from an early age the career they want to follow. Most take longer to decide. It's often difficult, especially when decisions need to be taken at the time of choosing GCSE options.

If you're sure of what you want to do, go for it. Motivation is perhaps your most positive asset. Never forget, though, that academic or vocational success isn't the only thing in life. Take time for relaxation, friends, family and fun. Most of all, for your relationship with God. That's the thing that will endure through life and beyond.

If you're not sure what you want to do, look around at all the possibilities. Despite recession and unemployment and other depressing things, the world is bursting with opportunities for young people, especially if they're Christians. Maybe this is the most exciting and challenging time there's ever been!

Don't be afraid to speak to the experts there to help you. Ask yourself what really interests you, what you enjoy and find fulfilling, where you feel you would fit. Don't panic if you still can't decide or if you think you've chosen the wrong course. You can always change channel. Ask for advice and help if you need it. Pray and ask for God's guidance in your career. He has a perfect plan for your life, just waiting for you to fit into it. Enjoy it!

Church

What is the church? Does the word 'church' make you think of that old grey stone building with a tower or a steeple that you pass every day on your way to school? Or the Sunday morning service you've gone to with your parents ever since you can remember? Or something else altogether?

Church buildings come in all shapes and sizes, from smart modern new-builds to small tin-roofed huts, from community centres to lofty cathedrals, from historic parish churches to village chapels, and lots in between.

But church isn't really about a building at all. The first church members in the days immediately after Jesus had gone back to heaven had no building but moved about from house to house for their church gatherings. The church is really all the people who have come to a relationship with Jesus Christ and committed their lives to him. However, most local gatherings of Christians have a place called church, where they meet regularly to worship and to share their lives with one another and with God. Christians are not meant to struggle along alone, but to be part of a family, the 'body' of Christ.

No family is perfect, and your church won't be perfect either, but each member needs the others, to encourage, to strengthen, to learn from, to correct when necessary, to belong to, to enjoy. And Jesus needs his church to make him complete. (Read Acts 2:36-42.)

Clothes

see also Fashion

Clothes are much more than a necessary covering or something to keep out the cold! Clothes make a statement to the world about the kind of person you are. What you wear will reflect who you are and how you feel about yourself, whether you're confident enough to develop your own style or whether you feel safer blending in and going with the flow; whether you go for what you know suits you or whether you follow every fashion fad, regardless of what it does to your less-than-perfect areas.

You're probably happiest in your jeans and tops, like most others of your age. You may or may not have hassle from your mum, who will have her own ideas of what looks good and what doesn't. They almost certainly won't coincide with yours. You probably think your mother has a very sad taste in clothes. However, she might have one or two very nice items in her wardrobe that you don't mind borrowing now and again. It's quite fortunate for you that she's put on a few pounds and can't borrow yours!

No doubt you feel that you'd like more clothes than you can afford. Swapping with your friends is a good idea. So are good charity shops. It's nice to have lots of options, though it does add to the time spent making that important decision about what to put on each day. You'll probably end up leaving a pile of discarded garments on your bedroom floor and go out on your usual jeans and top!

Complexes

A complex can develop from the most casual of remarks, even if no harm was intended and you know the person who made it is the most tactless you've ever met. It's so easy to pick up on a negative remark and let it blow up into something quite out of proportion.

Don't let the thoughtless words of someone else destroy your confidence. And make sure you help build up others with positive words.

Cooking
see also Diets, Food

Cooking is something that everyone should learn, male or female. Never pass up the chance of cookery classes, whether Cordon Bleu or simple basic stuff. They'll pay dividends in later life, maybe when you go to college or university, or to work away from home, not to mention when you have a home of your own. You'll probably learn anyway, by trial and error or from cookery books, but there are lots of short cuts and great ideas that make it all easier and the results more exciting.

Cooking, serving and eating a meal with friends is one of life's greatest pleasures. It's fun to make the table special with candles and flowers and your mum's best china. Try it as a way of introducing some of your favourite people to each other. Or just for some old friends. Or even Mum and Dad!

Cousins

Cousins are a strange breed, not quite siblings but not exactly mates either. You can't choose your cousins. They are forced upon you for better or worse, and you can't avoid meeting them at family gatherings.

Cousins are great when you're all small together. Remember those family occasions when the adults exchanged all the goss and put the world to rights, while a horde of cousins rampaged through the house (usually Grandma's) creating glorious havoc? Later, the older boy cousins grew long legs and deep voices, and the girls tended to giggle a lot or maybe gang up and get a bit bitchy. Never mind. They'll always be your cousins. And don't worry too much about being compared to that annoyingly pretty or clever cousin – it's just another irritating habit of the parent generation!

Cults

see also Religions

There are plenty of cults, sects and strange teachings around in this day and age, and sometimes it's difficult to sort out what's what. The fact that many Christians now meet in house groups, small fellowships and enquirer's groups, cell units and so on, makes it doubly confusing, especially for parents who may worry about just what it is their kids may be getting into. Their anxiety is understandable.

If you are a young Christian whose parents are concerned about you, the best way to reassure them is to invite them along to see just exactly what goes on in your youth club, church group or whatever else you may be involved in. All genuine leaders would welcome that kind of parental interest, and most have parents' evenings or special events when everyone can get to know each other.

Avoid like the plague any gathering that meets in secret or encourages you to break away from your family. Whatever they call themselves, these groups are not likely to be centred around Jesus.

As far as sound teaching goes, perhaps the most important question to ask is whether Jesus Christ is worshipped and acknowledged as the Son of God and the only means by which we can come into a right relationship with God. All true teaching must be centred around that. (Read Matthew 7:15-23.)

Dd

Death

No one likes to think about death. When we're young most of us tend to think that it will never happen to us. It's perhaps only when we lose someone close to us, a much-loved grandfather or grandmother or a friend, or when someone we know is killed in an accident, that we have to stop and face the fact of death.

Physical death happens to us all. It could be sooner or later; we don't know – and it's good that we don't. We do not, however, need to live our life under the shadow of the fear of death which is mentioned in the Bible. Jesus came to deliver us from that shadow, so that we can live our life in happy security.

We are told very clearly that anyone who knows and loves God will never die. Their body will perish but the real, vital person that we are will live on into a glorious eternity with God, where we will know happiness beyond our wildest dreams. Our destination after death can be settled now by knowing Jesus.

(Read 1 Corinthians 15:22.)

Decision Making

There are many decisions that have to be made in life. Perhaps the first big thing you'll have to decide is which subjects to take and which to drop at the beginning of your GCSE years. Then there'll be decisions about future study, colleges, the choice of a career and a life partner, your family and your lifestyle, and many more. Decisions have to be made at every stage of life, and sometimes it's hard to make the right ones. Friends and family can help. Even better, ask God to guide you at every stage where a decision has to be made.

Depression

Depression can hit at any age, and sometimes it's hard to recognise when it does. Most people are depressed at some time or other. Developing hormones can make for very up and down feelings in your teenage years. The odd down day is nothing to worry about and you'll probably feel better tomorrow.

On the other hand, if you (or a friend) have any of the following symptoms that aren't going away, it could be time to ask for help:

- lack of interest and enjoyment in life
- persistent tiredness and insomnia
- irritability and weepiness
- looking on the black side of everything
- being unusually nervous and worried

See your doctor, tell a trusted adult friend or a parent. There's plenty of help out there; don't be afraid to ask for it. Depression is horrid, but you'll come through it to laugh and enjoy life again.

Diets   *see also Cooking, Eating Disorders, Food*

A balanced diet is essential for proper growth and development, healthy skin and hair, alertness and energy. Your daily diet should include proteins, carbohydrates, fats, minerals and vitamins.

Crash diets are not a good idea. These put a strain on the body, the weight lost can be put back quickly, and the repeated yo-yo effect of weight loss and gain creates extra strain. Don't be taken in by the ultra-skinny models you see in magazines and on catwalks – that kind of look is not really attractive and certainly not healthy.

Skipping meals is not a good idea either, especially breakfast. Neither is stuffing yourself with junk food on a daily basis – it's OK once in a while. Try exercise as an alternative to dieting if you're not happy with your figure. Walking, jogging, cycling, swimming, dancing – all help to tone and condition the body, as well as burning up excess calories. Eating is one of the great pleasures of life, especially a meal with good friends. Thank God for the enormous range of available foods we have, and choose well from them.

Divorce

Divorce, sadly, is a fact of life in the age we live in. An increasingly high percentage of marriages are ending in divorce and broken homes.

God intended marriage to be for a lifetime, the loving commitment of a man and a woman to stay together for mutual support, comfort, sharing and enjoyment, and to bring up the children of the marriage in love and security.

We live in an imperfect world, all men and women are faulty beings, and this ideal all too often breaks down, even in Christian families. Divorce hurts everyone, not least the children. There are no winners. If your parents are divorced, you will have suffered because of it. It would be pointless to pretend otherwise.

But if you are a Christian, the love of Jesus in your life can make all the difference. Whichever parent was at fault (and it's not always as clear-cut as you may think), wherever you feel your sympathies lie, ask God to help you forgive them both. Resentment and bitterness do nothing but spoil your own life. Your parents are both hurting people and need your love and your forgiveness. Don't shut either of them out.

Apart from God, the pattern of broken marriage and divorce will often repeat itself in the next generation. With God, the pattern can be broken. In Christ all things are made new. With him at the centre of your life, you have every chance of meeting the life partner of his choice and achieving a happy and lasting marriage.

Doubt

We all have doubts, if we're honest. Doubts about our own worth, our abilities, relationships, just about everything. Even about God.

The strongest Christian has probably doubted God at some time or other. Doubted his ability to sort out an impossible situation, doubted that he really cares about us, or knows us, or answers our prayers. Doubted that he exists at all.

It's OK to have doubts. Don't pretend to be full of faith and confidence if you're not. Find a trusted older person, maybe in your family or at church, and talk to them about your doubts. Best of all, be honest with God and tell him about your doubts too.

Dreams

Dreams are strange things. Everyone dreams whenever they sleep, although they may not remember. Sleep experts reckon that dreams are necessary for our psychological and emotional health.

Some dreams may be strange or disturbing. Some may be astonishingly clear in detail. God sometimes uses dreams to tell someone something he wants them to know. If you feel this is the case, ask him what he is telling you.

Don't worry if nothing comes of it. Dreams can't hurt you. An upsetting one is probably just the result of that

late snack of cheese on toast that you ate before bed!
(A doctor friend told me that cheese really does encourage dreaming.)

Drugs

There are different types of drugs. Drugs are natural or chemical substances which, when used under medical supervision, can be used to treat many medical conditions and illnesses. Unfortunately, drugs are also subject to widespread abuse which can lead to addiction. This has resulted in deaths, chronic illness, ruined relationships, and spoiled potential of young lives.

Drugs can stimulate or depress the nervous system, produce delusions or hallucinations or feelings of euphoria, block out reality or even create the ability to perform unusual physical feats such as dancing non-stop for many hours. With this kind of activity, another danger can be severe dehydration and subsequent collapse, or even death.

Drug overdose can result in psychosis, convulsions, loss of consciousness and death. Drug users usually become dependent and long-term abuse can destroy a healthy body and mind. Users are liable to organ damage, malnutrition, mental illness, hepatitis, HIV (from dirty needles) and other infections.

It makes sense to avoid drugs completely, however harmless they may appear and however socially acceptable you might be encouraged to believe it is to take 'recreational drugs'.

If you're a Christian, pray for your friends who may be tempted into taking drugs. Be filled with the Holy Spirit who brings real joy and fulfilment, and show the world there's an alternative to the sad delusion of drugs.

Ee

Eating Disorders
see also Diets

There's a great deal of pressure for girls to have the right kind of figure, which, unfortunately, seems to mean thin. We are all different shapes and sizes. There is no ideal. If you are an average weight for your height and build and you feel well, don't be manipulated by pressure from the media, your friends or anything else.

Anorexia nervosa and bulimia nervosa are two disorders often connected with our perception of how we look. This can be misleading, though. Both these disorders are outward signs of something desperately wrong inside. Anorexics continue to lose weight by not eating enough, even when long past the point of acceptable slimness. Bulimics eat normally and then vomit up the food they've eaten. Sometimes they binge on large amounts before inducing vomiting, and they may use laxatives too. Acid from the stomach can seriously damage the digestive system, throat and teeth. Both anorexics and bulimics put their lives in serious danger.

The underlying problem is the thing that needs to be tackled. People with eating disorders need the will to want to get better. Recovery takes time.

If you feel you may have an eating disorder or are concerned for a friend, seek help. Be honest, face facts, pray and know that God cares and can help.

Embarrassment

So many things in life can be the source of embarrassment. Like teachers, or boys, or blushing, or families.

Families will behave in an embarrassing way when you take a new friend home for tea, especially if it's one you'd like to impress. Your little sister will giggle, your dad will blow his nose in that peculiar honking way, your grandma will insist on talking about when you were a baby, or, even worse, when your dad was a baby! Your brother's eating habits embarrass you, and so does the strange and sad outfit your mum has decided to wear. Even the dog will embarrass you by sniffing at your friend's ankles . . . or worse!

Going shopping with your mum can be seriously embarrassing. It's not just the sad outfit (another one) – it's her whole attitude. She doesn't know it's uncool to hold up dresses against you, or comment on them, or come into the changing room with you. She can't grasp that all she's required to do is wait quietly by the door and come forward with the Visa card when she's needed.

Seriously, embarrassment is common, but it loses its edge in time. Your confidence will grow and you'll gain assurance. You'll probably even stop blushing in time!

Environment

As humans we had a commission from our Creator God to care for the earth and everything in it. Sadly, we messed up. The greed and carelessness and apathy of humankind have all played a part in the disintegration of our world. Ultimately, there will be a new heaven and a new earth, with all things restored as God meant them to be.

In the meantime, we can all do something to help restore the harm that's been done and conserve the world's resources. We can recycle waste, plant trees, collect and campaign for good causes, clean up the countryside and polluted waterways. We can buy Fair Trade goods and find ways of helping the plight of war and famine victims, the homeless, underprivileged and exploited in our own and other societies.

Eternal Life
see also Death

Eternal life is God's gift to humankind which is freely available to us when we accept Jesus Christ as our Saviour and Lord.

It's hard to imagine a life that goes on for ever, with no time span, no limitations, no end. A life that is not bounded by physical problems, or social issues or space or need of any kind. It's mind-boggling! But it's what we can look forward to when this life is over, and you have to admit, that's fairly amazing!

The fear of death is something that hangs over every person ever born, to a greater or lesser degree. Whatever we achieve or gain in this life will come to an end one day. As an old song says, 'You can't take it with you when you go'.

Even our bodies will be left behind, like a garment we discard because we've outgrown it or it's worn out. But the real 'us', the personality which makes us who we are, goes on for ever.

We're not given many details of what we can expect in the next life. We read a few tantalising hints that there will be 'pleasures for evermore' and 'fullness of joy'. We will meet again loved ones who have died and we will see Jesus face to face.

Eternal life in heaven will be much more wonderful, fulfilling and joyful than anything our limited minds can imagine, and it all begins here and now. We are told that, in Jesus, we know that we have eternal life.

Evil

see also Sin

The world is a bad place and appears to be getting worse. Every day our newspapers and TV screens bear witness to the terrible things that go on. We do not need to detail them but we all have to admit that it's true.

The scene blackens. The Bible says that in the world the forces of evil will get worse and worse, until the time of the Lord's return.

Hopeless? A case for deep despair? No. The Bible says that Jesus is the light of the world. All of us who belong to him are walking in the light, and that the light will overcome the darkness. Let your light shine!

Exams

Exams are nerve-racking, whatever their level. The build-up to them – the research, the feverish revision, the striving to remember information that might be relevant – is equally stressful. Add to this the fact that many exams are held in early summer – peak time for hay fever – and it's a wonder that anyone ever passes anything.

You can minimise the strain. Eat proper meals at regular times, not snacks at midnight. Get plenty of sleep. (Midnight revision is not a good idea anyway.) Get some fresh air and exercise. Do your best on the day, but let God be in charge of the outcome, whatever it turns out to be. What matters is that you do your best . . . and relax!

Ff

Faith

Faith is something we all have a bit of. We use faith in all kinds of situations in everyday life, without even thinking about it. We have faith that a chair will bear our weight when we sit on it or that water will come out when we turn on the tap.

Faith in God is more difficult to define because we can't see God, but we all have a little of that sort of faith too. The Bible tells us that each of us is given a measure of faith. It's what we do with it that counts. Choosing to believe in Jesus, to take him at his word, will enable our faith to grow. The more we have faith, the more faith we'll have. (Read Hebrews 11:1-16.)

Families

see also Brothers, Cousins, Father, Grandparents, Mother, Parents, Sisters

Families come in many shapes and sizes these days. Gone is the time when a family consisted of a neat package of Mum, Dad and kids, with grandparents, aunts, uncles and cousins around the edges. Now a family is just as likely to include step-parents, step-brothers and sisters or half-siblings, not to mention combinations of grandparents and other connections. They may or may not be there all the time, they may share time with other families, and sometimes they only stay around for a while. It can be frustrating and confusing.

Often, though, it's possible to make good relationships with people who have joined our families at a later date in one way or another. Jealousy and rivalry can spoil these relationships and turn them sour; much better to take a positive view and value people for who and what they are in their own right. You may find you've gained some very good friends.

Fashion
see also Clothes

Fashions come and go. Often they come and go very fast indeed! Your mother may tell you she wore the same thing 25 years ago, but you are unlikely to be impressed with the limp garment she pulls from the back of the wardrobe.

Fashion is what hangs in racks in the high street boutiques and is being worn by everyone now, but the best fashion is your own particular style. Don't be led by the crowd!

Father

Every girl needs a father. A father is meant to be provider, protector, friend, defender, model of a man, comforter and (sometimes) judge. A father looks out for your interests at all times, and a good father would lay down his life for his child.

Not all fathers measure up to this ideal. Human fathers are, well, human. Some fathers are dysfunctional or absent. Some fathers never had fathers themselves and some fathers fail through no fault of their own.

God is the Father who never fails. He understands and loves each of his children unconditionally, whatever our situation, whatever our background, whatever we have done. He is the Father of those who have good human fathers and, particularly, he is the Father of the fatherless.

Fear
see also Nerves, Panic

Everyone has to cope with fear in one form or another. Fears range from nagging anxieties about your friendships, your future or something you have done, to fears about your family splitting up, fears of illness and fear of death. There are even the seemingly insignificant ones like fear of spiders or of the dark.

Fears that seriously limit our everyday lives could be described as neuroses or phobias. There are experts who can help us deal with these extreme fears.

Most fears can be overcome by bringing them out into the open and talking about them. Discuss your worries with someone you know and trust. If you go to a church or a youth group, get someone to pray with you. Fears seem to grow smaller when they are shared, and there's a good chance they'll shrink away altogether and disappear.

Figure

see Bras, Diets

Food

see also Cooking, Diets, Eating Disorders

Food is one of the great enjoyments of life, to be used well and wisely. We in the West have a great variety of foods to choose from. Sadly, much of it these days is of the 'junk' variety; fast food, takeaways, instant frozen foods. All convenient and time-saving, but don't forget to balance your diet with plenty of fresh foods, fruit, veg and salads, wholegrains and freshly-prepared home-cooked food. There's a long-overdue move towards healthy eating these days and it works out cheaper too. That's not to say we can't pig out occasionally, but better not to make a habit of it!

We can be thankful for the quality and abundance of our foods, but we mustn't be greedy or wasteful, bearing in mind that a great proportion of the world's people don't have enough to eat.

Football

see also Games

You either love football or loathe it. It's not everyone's idea of a brilliant weekend, shivering in the stands in a crowd of cheering, jeering, hollering, fanatical football fans. On the other hand, if you've been brought up with a dad/brothers/cousins who are players or avid supporters of a team, you'll probably be the most fanatical supporter of all.

Forgiveness

We need to forgive and be forgiven. We have forgiveness because Jesus took the punishment for our sins when he died on the cross. But we may still need to confess and ask forgiveness each time we are aware we have done wrong. Then, as far as God is concerned, it's all forgotten.

Forgiveness between fellow humans is important too. We may need to ask forgiveness of one another if we have said or done something we know to be wrong or hurtful. It may simply be because our attitude is wrong or that we've made a mistake. A sincere apology is the best way of melting away bad feeling and resentment. In the same way, we need to forgive others who have hurt or harmed us. Holding on to a grudge or seeking revenge will harm ourselves more than it harms the other person. There's freedom to be gained in letting go of anger and grudges. On the other hand, forgiveness doesn't necessarily mean that we must put ourselves in the position where we can be hurt in the same way again.

Gg

Games

see also Football

You may or may not be interested in traditional games of the sports variety – tennis, netball, hockey. If you are, great! Sport is a fantastic way of keeping fit, functioning as part of a team, making friends and working off surplus energy. If you're not sporty, how about board and card games (Chess, Monopoly, Trivial Pursuit, Pictionary, etc.)? They may seem completely uncool but it's surprising how much fun they can be, sometimes even more than computer games, where there's not much face-to-face interaction.

Gangs

Everyone needs their own circle of friends to hang out with. We all need to be known and accepted, to 'belong' in our particular group. The problems begin when rivalry rears its head, when a particular group feels it 'owns' an area or a style of dress, or a certain way of doing things, and resents it when others disregard the rules. Things can get out of hand pretty quickly. It's not showing loyalty to blindly follow your own 'gang' whether they're right or wrong. Better to use your head and work it out for yourself.

God

The most important decision you'll ever have to make concerns your personal relationship with God. You may or may not have grown up with people who believe in God and have committed their lives to him. Either way, you'll have to make up your own mind. Most people have thoughts about God that they may or may not share with others.

If you're searching for God, don't be afraid to ask. Speak to people you know are involved with church or youth groups. Read books. Find out other people's experiences. Ask questions. Best of all, try speaking to God for yourself, even if you're not quite sure about him. Tell him whatever is on your mind. He's not very far away and will be delighted to hear from you.

Going Out

'Going out' in your grandparents' day meant getting ready, being picked up or meeting someone at a certain time, actually going somewhere and arriving home (probably at a set time). It might have been a bit more relaxed in your parents' time, but it still meant actually going on a date.

Nowadays, going out seems to be less defined. It can be spending time, or hanging out with a special person, or it can mean that you have a certain kind of understanding with someone. It's a good idea to sort out what the expectations are before you agree to 'go out' with someone.

Grandparents

Grandparents are sometimes a pain, but can also be the biggest assets in the world. Grandparents are not directly responsible for you and so their attitude is fairly laid-back. Grandparents enjoy spoiling you with treats and presents when you are small, and slipping you a fiver or a tenner for something special when you are older. Grandparents brag about your accomplishments, turn a blind eye to your failings and laugh indulgently at your escapades (although your parents probably see to it that the very worst are kept from them). They beam with pride at your school plays, prize-givings and graduations, and boast about you in public to the point of embarrassment.

Grandparents may be elderly but they can be surprisingly understanding, tolerant or even broad-minded. They don't shock as easily as you might expect. They've got a lot of living under their belt and they're likely to have seen most of it before.

Groups

see Youth Groups

Hair

Can anything on earth be worse than a bad hair day? If your hair doesn't do what it's supposed to, your ends are split or you've got a fit of the frizzies, it can blight the sunniest morning or dampen the brightest mood. Some days, no amount of washing, conditioning, blowing and styling can make your hair look the way you want it to.

We all get those days. Maybe, though, we're the only ones who notice how awful our hair is.

A good diet is a must for healthy hair. So is regular washing in mild shampoo (too often or using products that are too harsh will strip hair of its natural oils), a good cut and a style that suits you. Deep conditioning will help dryness and is not too expensive.

Fashionable styles come and go, but one head of hair is all you'll get, so it pays to take care of it!

Health

For all its faults, we have one of the finest health services in the world, and all for free during school and student years. Good habits when you're young lay down a sound basis for a healthy life. It's cool to eat the right food, have vaccinations, medical and dental checks, and be aware of the dangers of alcohol and drug abuse and sexually transmitted diseases. Everyone needs some kind of exercise and enough sleep. Good habits started early can go a long way to ensuring a lifetime of good health.

Holidays
see also Travel

Holidays can be fantastic fun or they can be the pits. It depends a lot on what you make of them. You can be miserable in Miami or have a great time in Great Yarmouth.

Maybe the best holidays are when you're with a group your own age with similar interests. Christian camps, house parties, youth conferences, even summer projects or mission outreach, can be among the most rewarding and amazing times of your life. You'll strengthen existing friendships, make rewarding new ones, and probably want to book up straight away for next year.

Family holidays can be a bit more tricky, especially when there's a wide diversity of age groups. You may feel bored or restricted if there are people much older or younger than you to be considered. Try not to moan too much. It's not much fun for anyone else being stuck with a moody teenager. Your mum wants you to be happy and is probably working her socks off to make sure all of you have a good time. You might even find that you do!

Holy Spirit

The Holy Spirit is the third person of the Trinity. He is the Spirit of Jesus, sent by him after he had ascended back to his Father in heaven. The Holy Spirit comes to live within every believer when they commit themselves to God through faith in Jesus Christ.

The Holy Spirit is likened to fire, wind, oil, water and a dove. He came with great power at the first Pentecost and transformed the lives of the first Christians. He is available in the same way to transform lives today.

Any Christian can receive this filling of the Holy Spirit simply by asking for it. It can be helpful to do this within a group of mature and trusted Christians. We read in the Bible that the Spirit-filled Christian bears fruit in his or her life: love, joy, peace, patience, kindness, goodness, faithfulness, humility and self-control. The Holy Spirit also gives the gifts of wisdom, knowledge, faith, healing, miracle working, prophecy, tongues and interpretation, to be used for the benefit of others as well as the recipient.

The Holy Spirit can be grieved if we reject him in our life, and his working can be quenched if we do not obey. (Read 1 Corinthians 14: 13-20.)

Home

There is an old saying that home is the place where you behave your worst and are treated the best. Maybe it's not far wrong. In a good home, you will feel free to let your hair down, show your feelings, freak out if you need to, just be yourself. You can't pull the wool over the eyes of the people you live with anyway. You will be tolerated and forgiven in a way that would happen nowhere else.

Home is another of those things that is largely what you make it. It can be a haven or it can be hell on earth. We do well to thank God for our homes and make them the best we possibly can.

Homelessness

Every year, hundreds of young people make the decision to run away from home. Their reasons for doing so can range from serious abuse within the home to something as minor as an argument about clothes or boyfriends or being found out in some deception. Most will head for a big city, believing that here they will find 'freedom', but in reality they are exposing themselves to the most horrendous risks.

Some young people even kid themselves that their parents will be better off without them – most seem completely unaware of the total devastation and heartbreak that is caused when a child goes missing.

Many young people regret their hasty decision when they find how scary and threatening it is to have left behind home and security. Jobs are not out there waiting for them and a safe place to live is almost impossible to find. Plenty of people are on the lookout for vulnerable youngsters to take advantage of. A lot of runaways would like to return home but are afraid of getting into more trouble, having more restrictions placed upon them or of feeling a failure.

The vast majority of parents would be more likely to react as the father of the Prodigal son did, so great would be their relief to get their child back. (Read Luke 15:11-31.)

Homework

It's a drag, isn't it? And possibly the last thing you feel like doing after a hard day at school. All you want to do is relax, hang with friends, chat online, watch TV, listen to music or just crash out. It's a necessary evil, though, and best tackled and got out of the way as soon as possible, maybe after a snack and a short rest. Your conscience is then clear and you have a bit of time to yourself. Storing up weekend homework for a last frantic effort on Sunday evening is not a good idea either.

Hormones   *see also Depression, Periods*

Hormones are responsible for a lot of aggro during your teenage years. The onset of puberty, with its release of hormones into the bloodstream, is responsible for the normal body changes as you become an adult – breast development, the growth of body hair, the start of periods.

This process can also be blamed for mood changes, tiredness, hyperactivity, and other ups and downs. All this is normal and things will settle down again before too long. You are not going through a personality change, and neither are the people around you, although it may be a difficult time for everyone.

Unfortunately, hormone activity in a teenage girl can sometimes coincide with the other end of the scale – a mother approaching menopause. You will both need a little extra TLC, tact and understanding, and maybe your own space and privacy from time to time.

Hypocrisy

Your generation is probably a bit less hypocritical than previous generations. You are not afraid to ask questions and demand answers, you do not put on an act to please your elders, and you will not suffer those who say one thing and do another.

As far as your faith in God is concerned, you will not be satisfied with something handed down from your parents, but must find and experience truth for yourself.

This is great, and God will honour those who are honest with him and with themselves. However, please don't be too harsh with those who don't know all the answers or who seem to fall short in some way. The most sincere and mature Christians are only human and can make mistakes now and then. (Read Matthew 21:28-32.)

Ii

Ideals

It's easy to be idealistic, to see things in terms of black and white, right and wrong. Our ideals don't always coincide with those of our parents' generation, however. We need to have ideals, something that we aim for and aspire to. It's probable, though, that our sights will change as we grow older, that black and white will change to shades of grey, that some of our ideals will be impossible to realise. Disillusionment can set in, but with God in our lives we can acknowledge our own weakness and allow him to work his purposes in us and for us.

Idols

Idols don't have to be statues, images or carved figures. They can also be pop stars, boyfriends, footballers, supermodels, some prized possession or our own ambition – anything that takes the place of God in our life. God's word states very clearly that he must take first place in our life, and that, like all his commands, this is for our own good.

Individual

There's a lot of pressure to follow the trend, to be part of the crowd. It stems from a basic need to be accepted and loved. We need to remind ourselves that God has created us as individual beings. No two are exactly alike. There's never been another person exactly like you in the world's history and there never will be. You are a unique individual, a one-off. God broke the mould when he made you! So, let's not try too hard to be like everyone else, or even like anyone else. Let's rejoice in the things we have in common and in our differences too.

Internet

You will have grown up with the internet, an 'internet native' as opposed to those 'internet immigrants' who had to learn it all! Most of today's communication is done by means of the internet. So is a great deal of research, homework, buying and selling, checking out new stuff, looking at pictures and videos and, of course, socialising. Most of you will belong to a group such as Facebook, Bebo or MySpace, or you may have your own blog. These are fine, a good way of keeping in touch and lots of fun, if addictive and a bit time-wasting.

A few words of warning, though – time spent in front of the screen can take you away from real socialising with real people. More seriously, there are people on the lookout for young and vulnerable people. Never link up with people unless you know them or have been introduced by someone else. There's status in having lots of 'friends' on your list, but don't fall for the idea of adding someone to make up the numbers. It may be better not to post an actual recent photo of yourself – you can put up one of your baby days, or your cat or dog, or any kind of fun picture. Don't forget that anyone on your list of friends, or on their lists, can look you up too. And never give out certain personal details – phone numbers (home or mobile), address, or even the school you go to or the events you plan to attend. There have been plenty of cases of internet stalkers who can pose a real threat. Don't ever be tempted to arrange to meet someone you don't know and watch out for scams. Stay safe.

Jj

Jealousy

Jealousy is a real nasty! It nags away at your mind, it ties your stomach into knots and generally messes up your life. Maybe you're jealous of a brother or sister who you think gets more time, attention or privileges than you do. Or someone your age who is prettier or cleverer, or who attracts the guys who don't seem to notice you at all.

Being jealous is a dead loss and a real waste of time and energy. It doesn't get you anywhere and gives you a load of ugly, spiteful, negative feelings you're better off without. The person you're jealous of has probably got plenty of problems and hang-ups too. They may even be jealous of you!

Friendships and family relationships are, humanly speaking, probably the most important things in life. Don't let them be spoiled by jealousy. (Read Psalm 37.)

Jesus

Jesus Christ is the central figure of the whole Christian faith. He is part of the Trinity of Father, Son and Holy Spirit. He is fully God, yet he became human and lived an ordinary life on earth in order to share our experiences, our joys and sorrows and sufferings. He died on the cross to take the punishment for our sins, so that we can go free. He rose from the dead so that we can have victory over death. He went back to his Father in heaven, and sent us his Spirit to fill us and help us in our life.

He is described as our saviour, priest, prophet, friend, king and husband! He loves us all and wants us to be with him for eternity. Isn't that amazing!

Jobs
see also Work

It's good to have a Saturday or holiday job. You'll learn a bit about what it's like to go to work and get a lot of experience of dealing with people and working alongside others. You may even land up with something that helps you decide on your future career – even if it's something you find you definitely don't want to do! Best of all, you'll have some cash of your own and won't have to be so dependent on stingy pocket money and hand-outs from hard-up parents!

Kissing

Kissing can be a big worry (that is, kissing a boy) especially if you haven't done much (or any) of it before. The simple snog seems fraught with problems. Who should you kiss? How exactly do you do it? How long should a kiss last? What happens to the noses?

Don't worry about it. Kissing is no big deal, and there's no formula for doing it. You could practise by puckering up in front of a mirror but you'll waste a lot of time and won't gain much. A kiss with someone you trust and are genuinely fond of will happen spontaneously when the time is right.

Ll

Late Nights

You probably get a lot of hassle about late nights. Everyone wants to stay out as late as their friends do, and think's it's unreasonable of parents to object. Don't they understand you'll be just fine?

The trouble is, they don't. To a teenager, parents are hopelessly out of touch, their idea of a late night being to stay up until 11.30pm watching a schmaltzy movie with a mug of cocoa. However, they object because they care. They're concerned not only for your safety but for your health, your well-being, your happiness and your future. That's why they make rules. Try and talk it over and come to an agreement that's acceptable to all parties. And thank God for parents who care.

Lending

There are two sides to lending. It's a great drag when your younger sister wants to borrow your new top, bike, make-up or latest DVD. You know without doubt it'll come back creased, dented, used-up or scratched. Or not come back at all.

On the other hand, it seems perfectly reasonable to borrow your big brother's bike, or his funky new shirt, or his tennis racket. And he really doesn't need to be such a pain, complaining that it's damaged, or crumpled, or mislaid . . .

Loneliness

It's possible to be lonely, even in a crowd. It's lonely when people aren't on your wavelength, like when you're the only Christian in your year. It's lonely when you're revising for exams and everyone else seems to be out enjoying themselves. It's lonely when you feel misunderstood. It's lonely when you move to a new home, a new school, a new situation and don't know anyone, and everyone else seems to fit into some tight little group. Even family holidays can be lonely when there's no one else your age to talk to.

Wallowing in self-pity doesn't really help. Why not look for someone else who might be lonely too and make the first move towards getting to know them?

Love

Love is . . .

Well, it's many things. It's growing up in a warm, close family who care for you. It's finding a special friend, of either sex, with whom you have things in common, whom you trust and who you know will always be there for you.

It's meeting that special person and experiencing those heart-stopping, stomach-churning, spine-tingling, pulse-quickening emotions that are associated with falling in love. It's getting to know someone, finding that you 'click' in the way you think, or view the world, or laugh at things. It's learning to care, and especially to care as much about the other person's needs as about your own. It's being secure enough to be able to reach out and love others without being afraid of getting hurt ourselves. Love is belonging.

Perhaps the best description of love is given in the New Testament. (1 Corinthians 13.)

Magazines

The shelves are full of magazines specially aimed at the teenage girl. Generally speaking, they're a mix of true-life confession-type stories, cartoons, music and fashion, readers' letters and agony-aunt advice. There's always heavy emphasis on pop stars and groups, celebrity gossip, comments on the lives of people in the TV reality shows and so on, and a lot of emphasis on boy/girl concerns. Some magazines do try to make an effort to be responsible, but take care. The majority don't reflect a Christian world-view. There are some excellent Christian mags about, though. Most of them are cool and bang up-to-date, and can be a real help in maintaining Christian standards in the wider world.

Make-Up

Your mother probably tells you that you don't need to use make-up as you have a young skin, fresh complexion, good colouring, etc.

You just know that you need every bit of help you can get to disguise your all-too-apparent faults, or to improve on what God saw fit to hand out to you in the way of looks.

Make-up can't work miracles, but it sure can help! It's a bit sad to slap it on with a trowel, though. Better to find out what suits you, your colouring and skin-type. A makeover can be a good laugh, maybe with a friend to share it as a birthday treat. You'll come out feeling like a million dollars, your confidence will get a boost and you'll probably learn a lot too. But always remember – it's not the make-up that makes you beautiful but who you are! (Corny, but true!)

Marriage

The idea of marriage can produce mixed feelings. Many young people today feel that marriage is outdated and that it's a commitment that's impossible to live up to. Doesn't it make more sense to live together and see how it goes?

In God's eyes, marriage is a serious commitment that two people make to one another. He sets a high standard on the state of marriage, likening it to the union between Christ and his Body, the Church. There's arguably no such thing as a perfect marriage – after all, we're all faulty human beings – but it's an ideal worth striving for and working towards. The Church of England wedding service states that the purposes of marriage are for mutual care, comfort and encouragement, and to provide a secure environment for the nurture and upbringing of children.

There is no doubt that a secure, committed marriage, even one with faults, is the best setting for raising children to be stable and balanced individuals. Like any institution, a marriage will go through change, growth and necessary adjustment as it matures. There needs to be flexibility, tolerance, kindness and plenty of humour, but a good marriage can last a lifetime and be the greatest blessing of all.

Mistakes   *see also Reputation*

Everyone makes mistakes. Some don't matter, although we could kick ourselves at the time. Others can have far-reaching consequences. Once a mistake is made, it can't usually be reversed but we can react positively to our mistakes by learning from them and, hopefully, by not making the same mistake twice.

Money

Most of us feel we could do with a bit more money. There's never quite enough for all we feel we need or want, to buy or to do.

It's good to have a way of earning some extra money, from a Saturday job, or baby-sitting, or even helping out in extra ways at home. Making a little bit of money go a long way can be a challenge and it can be good fun too. Charity shops, jumble sales and car boot sales are all good hunting grounds. And when you're tired of the things you have, you could always get together with friends and have your own sale. It's also rewarding to give something away, however little it may seem, to a charity or to someone in need. Give it a try, you could be pleasantly surprised.

Moods

 see Hormones

Mother

It's said that the most intense relationship in the human experience is that of a mother and her daughter. It could well be true. The daughter's growing-up time can be traumatic for both. A mother wants to protect her daughter from the heartaches she may have suffered herself. A daughter is determined to go her own way and make her own mistakes. A mother sometimes resents the fact (maybe subconsciously) that her daughter is growing into an attractive woman, while a daughter feels that her mother thinks she knows everything. Mothers and daughters can be good friends, but they can also have spectacular rows, the kind of screaming matches that send the menfolk heading for the door.

Things will settle down and even out. You will probably discover you have a lot in common. A daughter dreads growing up to be like her mother, but by the time she does the two of them will probably be the best of friends.

Moving

Moving home is one of the most traumatic happenings in life. It can be fun, challenging and stimulating, settling into a new home, new school, new church, making new friends and meeting new people.

It can also mean a painful pulling-up of roots, leaving special mates or beloved grandparents, being forced to mix with people who speak, work and worship differently, finding your way about a new neighbourhood and learning to fit in.

Moving isn't always easy, but you will adjust and find your feet. Joining something like an evening class, a sports club or youth fellowship is a good start.

Music

Music is important, whatever kind you're into. It's one of the great creative gifts, often helping to express feelings that can't find expression any other way.

Your parents' taste and your own will probably be poles apart during your teen years. In bygone days this could cause serious tension when loud music reverberated through the house and offended parental eardrums. Nowadays, thank goodness, there is the iPod.

Nn

Nail-Biting

We'd all love to have long, glossy, varnished, well-shaped fingernails. Those stumpy, bitten, miserable little appendages to fingers owned by nail-biters do tend to spoil the image.

Nail-biting is usually a nervous thing, worse in times of stress. You may have the willpower to abstain for a while, but sudden anxiety or some major pressure-point can have you reducing those sprouting nails to their former sad, chewed, down-to-the-quick state in no time.

Painting the nails with a nasty-tasting substance can help. At the very least it reminds you of what you are doing. Invest in a stunning new shade of nail varnish, or post a picture of a beautiful pair of hands complete with long, strong, unbitten nails where you can't miss seeing them.

Names

Who doesn't, at some time or other, hate the name they were landed with by their well-meaning parents? Who were they to decide, anyway? I mean, how could they tell we were going to grow into a Victoria or an Abigail but not a Kylie or a Cleo or a Kate?

In their defence, they had to name us something and couldn't very well keep addressing us as 'hey, you!' until we were old enough to choose our own names. So they probably did the best they could in the circumstances.

Most of us get used to our names or even grow attached to them in time. Even if we really hate our name, it can usually be shortened or adapted in some way. To our mates, we'll usually be Abs or Caz or Becs anyway.

Nerves
see also Depression, Fear, Panic

Nearly everyone suffers from some degree of 'nerves' at certain times, such as important exams, interviews, taking part in plays or performances, facing new situations or meeting new people. Nerves can affect us with just a necessary flow of extra adrenalin to help us perform, or they can cause horrid stomach-knotting, trembling, paralysing feelings.

Some form of relaxation is good for someone suffering badly from nerves. Allow plenty of time to get ready for the event so that you don't have to rush. Don't forget to eat, even if you feel you couldn't swallow a mouthful. Try to take a few minutes to breathe deeply. Pray about the problem, and ask someone else to pray for you too.

Normal

What is normal? Is there such a thing?

Many people have unnecessary worries about what is normal or what isn't. God has created us with such a diversity of looks, sizes, colours, shapes, abilities, personalities, talents and characteristics that it's impossible to describe what is normal. Something that is unacceptable in one culture may be perfectly acceptable in another and considered normal.

Christian standards of normality are often different from those of the world. If you are worried, talk to someone you trust who is older and more experienced. And remember, whatever your differences, the chances are that you are every bit as normal as anyone else.

Oo

Occult

Meddling with the occult is dangerous and should be avoided at all costs, however exciting it may seem. The word 'occult' simply means 'hidden', and we are commanded by God to have nothing to do with the hidden works of darkness. Even things which may seem harmless fun – fortune tellers, horoscopes or playing with Ouija boards – can be dangerous, so the best advice is simply to leave well alone.

Ozone Layer

see Environment

Panic

see also Fear, Nerves

'Don't panic!' is easy to say but not so easy to put into practice when you're faced with a sudden danger or situation that makes your mouth go dry, your heart race and your arms and legs feel frozen to the spot. It might be real danger or it might be the unexpected sight of someone who's just broken your heart, out with his new girlfriend, or it could be anything in between. A few deep breaths will calm you. If you feel faint, clench your fists half a dozen times to return blood to the brain and sit down.

Parents

see also Father, Mother

Parents can be a mixed blessing. A person in their teens will probably have more confrontations with a parent/parents than anyone else.

They seem to exist solely to prevent you from doing/going/wearing the things/places/gear you wish to. They don't give you credit for any common sense, intelligence or integrity. They don't understand what it is to be young.

On the other hand, it's worth reflecting that parents are also the people who feed, clothe, house and nurture you, and pay the bills. Above all, they care. And they go on caring, no matter how much grief you give them. They have feelings. They may not be so cool, but parents are people too. (Read Exodus 20:12.)

Parties

We all love parties. Or do we? At a party we can relax, get to know new people, socialise, have a laugh and generally chill. A good party has food and drink, cool people, music and fun.

The downside is that parties can be scary if you don't know many other people, or if you feel you don't fit in, or if you think people might laugh at you when you get up to dance. And at some parties there may be pressure to drink too much, do drugs, or engage in sexual activity. That kind of party is bad news and best avoided.

Having your friends around to party the night away while your parents are out or away is not too clever either. You'll be stressed out trying to keep things under control, and it's hardly worth the music you'll have to face when they find out.

Peer Pressure

see also Individual

When everyone else is doing something or going somewhere, it's very tough to be the only one who's not. Each of us needs to belong and to feel accepted as part of the crowd. It's no fun standing outside looking in.

So peer pressure is a strong influence and not to be underestimated. Many a person has given in against their better judgement, whether the pressure is about drugs, alcohol, casual sex, dishonesty or any number of other things that may seem attractive but are ultimately destructive. Nor can we assume that those people who pressured us will stand by us and support us when we begin to suffer the consequences of our actions. Sadly, they're likely to be the first to desert us and add insult to injury by talking about us behind our back.

God doesn't intend us to stand alone, or to fight major battles all on our own. He knows it's hard to be a young Christian in today's hostile world. There are others facing the same pressures and together, we can be strong enough to overcome. The Bible says that we are to encourage one another, pray for each other, and bear one another's burdens. (Read Galatians 6:1-2.)

Periods

Periods are a pain, and that's not meant to be a joke. Those times of the month used to be called 'the curse' and it's not hard to understand why! It's a drag having to spend time being moody, tired, out-of-sorts, and prone to all kinds of physical ills from stomach cramps to spots. Having to postpone meaningful life for days every single month is just not fair! Guys just don't know how lucky they are!

There are all kinds of things available to help with painful periods or PMT, and most difficulties seem to settle down as girls grow older. Many girls in their teens have irregular periods, and these usually even out, given time. There's a great diversity in the age individual girls begin their periods, from as early as nine or ten up until sixteen or seventeen. A lot depends upon body weight, and family history plays a part too. Most variations are likely to be perfectly normal, but if you're worried, talk to a professional medical person, if only to set your mind at rest.

Perspective

Events and circumstances, especially distressing ones, can make you feel that the bottom has dropped out of your world. Disappointments, failures, let-downs, break-ups; these can completely floor you and make you feel that nothing will ever be the same again.

Wait a bit before you completely despair. They say time is a great healer and it's true. Pains ease, things do become more bearable. You won't forget the traumas, but you can learn from them and you can become stronger as a result. You may understand why things happened as they did. You may even be allowed to see God's hand at work in the situation. Things look very different when viewed in perspective.

Prayer

In prayer, we have one of the greatest resources available to the Christian. We can reach God in prayer at any time, in any place, whatever our need, situation, circumstances or state of mind. In Old Testament times, prayer had to be made through a priest at special times, but since Jesus came we have direct access to God, always.

God loves us to speak to him in prayer. Nothing we can say to him will shock him, upset him, anger him or cause him to love us less. Nothing we can ask is too hard for him to fulfil. If we are bewildered or confused, he understands. If we're angry, he doesn't mind us shouting at him. If we're desperate, he wants to hear from us so that he can begin to do something about it. He wants to hear about it when things are going well, too, and share in our delights. We are his children, he's interested in the tiniest details of our life, and he wants to be involved. (Read 1 Timothy 2:8.)

Pregnancy

Pregnancy, sadly, is an all too real fact of life for many girls in their teens. All of us will know someone who has got pregnant at an early age. Pregnancy may be physically possible from the age of puberty, but a young girl is far from ready for the changes and responsibilities that the prospect of becoming a parent involves. A girl is still growing and developing, physically, mentally and emotionally, until her late teens, and needs to be able to complete her own growing before being fully able to sustain another life. Babies need two parents, and young teenage girls are unlikely to have a partner who is mature enough to share in the responsibility of providing and caring for a child. Neither can a girl's own parents be expected to share the load – they've done their share of child-raising. A new life is a gift from God and needs to be well planned and prepared for.

Girls may have a lot of mistaken ideas of what it's like to have a baby. They may feel that a baby will give them that unconditional love they need; sadly, a newborn is totally self-centred and demanding 24/7, and won't be able to give much in return for a long time. A baby needs total attention, whether you're exhausted, desperate for sleep, longing to see your friends, or just fed-up. Girls who've tried the experiment of caring for a demanding dummy baby for a day or two have found it a real eye-opener.

Another myth is that if you're a single mum you'll automatically get a flat of your own – it just doesn't happen like that.

Privacy

see also Bedrooms

A bit of privacy does not seem much to ask, but as far as your family's concerned, it seems like asking for gold. Your younger siblings consider it their right to burst into your room at any time and help themselves to your belongings, borrow anything they fancy, and rifle through your cupboards. Even your mum, you suspect, has a quick sift through your personal effects when she comes in to collect the laundry or empty the wastepaper bin. Your sister earwigs your private conversations if she gets half a chance and your brother sneakily peers over your shoulder and sniggers when you're chatting online. If you ask for a lock on your door, your dad gets suspicious (what does he think you do in there, for goodness' sake?) and your mum worries about the fire hazards of locked doors. All in all, it's easier to go to the public library if you want a bit of peace and quiet. Either that, or lock yourself in the garden shed.

Protection

We live in an increasingly difficult society where safety can no longer be taken for granted. Everyone needs to be aware of the dangers and to avoid those places and gatherings where violence could erupt. Given the tragic increase in knife crime, some people believe that carrying a knife themselves can give protection. This is not the case, in fact, it's been proved that those carrying knives are more likely to be victims of attack. A police-type whistle or similar alarm makes more sense, along with staying clear of trouble spots, and staying in groups and with people you trust.

Qq

Quarrels

see Rows

Questions

It is good to ask questions. How else are we meant to find out things we don't understand? Parents, teachers, pastors, youth leaders and other responsible adults are the best people to ask, and are usually delighted to answer your questions. Maybe it's not too clever to exclusively consult others our own age – or at any rate don't lay any bets on getting correct answers! They may be just as much in the dark themselves, though they might not admit it.

God doesn't mind us questioning him either, even if we have our doubts and reservations about him. Reading the New Testament gospel accounts of the life and teachings of Jesus can answer a lot of our questions about the reality and nature of God. (Grab a Bible and have a look through either Matthew, Mark, Luke or John.)

Rebelling

A degree of rebellion is a pretty common part of growing up. Suddenly a young person becomes aware that he or she is no longer a child, and begins to question and kick against parental rules and regulations. That's OK – a developing identity needs to test the boundaries, to see what happens when they decide not to conform, and to experience the result of taking control of their own life. A certain amount of rebellion is inevitable, and even a healthy sign of normal development.

But it can all easily get out of hand. It's often confusing for both child and parents, and sometimes downright painful. Happily, most teenage rebellion is short-lived and the dust settles again, maybe in a new pattern, but hopefully one that is acceptable to all parties.

Prolonged rebellion, as in the story of the Prodigal son, is a heartbreaking business and often a sign of stored-up resentment. God's heart aches when his beloved children rebel against him, but, like the father in the parable, he waits eagerly with open arms for the rebellious one to return. (Read Luke 15: 11-24.)

Relationships

see also Boyfriends

Relationships (meaning the boy/girl variety) are a main preoccupation with all young people and often cause a lot of aggro. Everyone needs someone to be close to and to share with. Parents do not always realise the seriousness of teenage relationships, or the depth of pain involved when one comes to an end. You may be young, but things can hurt just as much as when they happen to older people. Remarks like 'There are plenty more fish in the sea' seldom help much, especially when the only fish you're remotely interested in has swum away leaving you high and dry.

A friend with a sympathetic ear and shoulder is usually the biggest comfort when things aren't going so well. And time, and prayer, and not being in too much of a hurry to look for another relationship.

Religions

see also Cults

You will rub shoulders with many people of other religions in today's multi-cultural society. The increasing practice in most schools is to include all religions in their acts of worship.

The religious faiths of other people are to be respected. It serves no purpose to zealously denounce any belief that is not our own, or to constantly criticise and point out its failings. On the other hand, we need to remember that the only way to God is through acceptance of Jesus Christ as our Saviour and Lord. A hotch-potch of doctrines picked from other religions, however attractive, will not do.

Christ is the living Saviour who changes lives, not just a religion of rules and rituals and ideals. By his Holy Spirit, we can live a life that stands out, so that others notice, and hopefully, want to know more.

Reputation   *see also Individual, Peer Pressure*

Once lost, a reputation cannot usually be regained very easily. There are people who watch your every move and need no encouragement to blacken your name. Best not to provide fuel, even a little bit. Respect yourself and stay away from anything you know to be wrong and harmful. Mud sticks.

However, memories are short and others will probably forget before you do. If you've done wrong, ask God's forgiveness, forgive yourself, and ask God to help you forgive others.

Rows

Most people fall out with someone else from time to time. Most often, it'll be someone we're close to, a family member or a friend. It wouldn't be human nature if everyone agreed with everyone else, all the time.

Just the same, rows and quarrels can be upsetting, especially if they go on and on, and involve people taking sides. It's childish and silly to sulk and refuse to speak to someone you've fallen out with. OK, so you're hurting and you feel it was the other person's fault and therefore their place to say sorry first; they probably feel exactly the same. No one wants to be the first to apologise, and the rift gets wider. It's cool to have the guts to make the first move, and you'll probably be pleasantly surprised at the results.

Rules

Rules are made to be broken, or so the saying goes. Rules are also laid down for a purpose, usually the protection and well-being of those asked to abide by them. Sticking to the rules will not necessarily cramp your style. In fact, you may find that in doing so you will gain trust and, in the long run, greater freedom.

Ss

School

see also Teachers

A person spends on average, twelve to fourteen years at school, not counting college or university. That's a good slice out of your life.

You may love school or hate it. It may seem the ultimate in restriction or the greatest opportunity and challenge. You may be in a well-ordered private school or a concrete jungle, or anywhere in between.

It really does pay off to work at school. Although missed opportunities can always be taken up later, our school years are the time when our brain and intellect are best able to absorb and retain information, and the time when we're free of other responsibilities, such as earning a living or maintaining a home and family. We have the freedom to follow our dreams and the means to work towards realising them. Schools have technology and resources freely available for our use, and support and encouragement to pursue the studies of our choice. School provides lasting friendships and can offer support when things may be difficult at home or elsewhere. Sadly, we maybe value our schooldays most when we have moved on to the more challenging environments of college or university, or out into the big wide world.

Self-Esteem

There are some strange ideas around about self-esteem, even in Christian circles. We may have been told not to be big-headed or to have too high an opinion of ourselves, or had it impressed upon us that we should always put others first. (A tall order!)

We're not meant to be inordinately full of ourselves, but being unnaturally humble is not what self-esteem is all about either. We're probably only too aware of our faults and failings, never mind the put-downs that life often throws at us. Maybe we need to see ourselves as God sees us.

Each one of us is precious to God, a unique creation designed and made by him, and he loves us just the way we are. It's been said though, that he loves us too much to leave us the way we are. As soon as we decide to follow Jesus, he's in the business of transforming us into the kind of people he intended us to be in the first place.

God wants us to remember how much he cares for us, and to respect ourselves accordingly. We may be born sinners, but we are now covered with the righteousness of Jesus. We're OK people in God's eyes and we need to be able to reckon ourselves valuable in order to be able to reckon others. (Read Matthew 10: 29-31.)

Sex

God created us male and female, and approved of the differences! His view was that he'd done a very good thing. He'd given us sex as a wonderful gift, to be used and shared and enjoyed within the security and commitment of lifelong marriage.

The gift of sex has been cheapened and exploited and altered from God's original plan. The sex drive is a powerful human force and is seen everywhere in today's society – in movies, magazines, TV, advertising. Sex sells. Often it is a distorted, over-emphasised and misleading view of sex. This cheapening and distortion has ruined lives and shattered relationships, a tragic result of ignoring God's laws concerning the use of sex.

As Christians, we need to stand firm and not to be drawn into the values and moral standards of this fallen world. It's easy to go with the crowd, but even more worthwhile waiting to share sex with that special person who is to be your chosen life partner. (Read Matthew 5: 27-37, John 8:1-11, 2 Samuel 11:1-15.)

Shopping

Most of us find there's nothing like a bit of 'retail therapy' for cheering up a fit of the blues. A new top or pair of jeans can put a spring back in the step and a sparkle in the eye, even if they're only from the local street market.

There's a lot of good value for money stuff around these days. Be aware though, of how some of the cheap clothing is produced (child labour, pitifully small wages, poor working environment) and shun those retailers who buy from these sources.

It makes a difference who you go shopping with, of course. Shopping with your mum is usually a definite no-no, and other relatives for company aren't too cool either. Neither is a boyfriend the best person to shop with – just notice how many fellas there are hanging round the doorways of High Street boutiques on Saturday mornings, blocking the way and looking bored!

The best shopping companion is perhaps your best friend, especially if she's honest enough to tell you that the little strappy top you fancy so much tends to turn your complexion to the colour of mud, makes your upper arms look gigantic and will probably lose its shape in the very first wash! After all, what are friends for?

Sin

see also Evil

We don't like to talk about sin, do we? It's not at all comfortable to face up to the fact that we're all sinners, but we only have to look at the world around us to know it's true. The human race has messed up, and it's all down to sin in the human heart.

There's a remedy though. God sent his Son into the world to live a sinless human life and so be able to become a perfect sacrifice for all our sin. Because of him, we can go free, our sins forgiven and forgotten. With Jesus in our life, we can make a real difference to a sick and sinful world.

Sisters

Your sister may be your best friend or your worst enemy. Your feelings may also be quite ambiguous – maybe you're the best of mates one minute and at each other's throats the next. It's not always easy being a sister, especially if you have to share a room. Often that spills over into sharing other things like clothes, make-up, books, hairdryers, computers – sometimes voluntarily but too often without permission from the other, resulting in more rows. Your sister usually knows you very well. It may be possible to pull the wool over your parents' eyes but not your sister's. And she also knows just which buttons to push to wind you up!

On the other hand, when life is getting you down and all other comfort fails, your sister will probably be the one who's there for you with a comforting shoulder and a big box of tissues.

Smoking

Smoking and its effects kills more people than all other addictions put together – fact! Sadly, it is more widespread among teenage girls than boys. Smoking is closely linked with lung cancer, from which there are 100,000 deaths per year. Some of these will not even be smokers, but will have suffered the results of inhaling other people's cigarette smoke. Smoke also clings to clothes, hair, and furnishings, changes breath and body odour, stains teeth, dulls hair and skin.

It's no longer allowed to smoke in public places, but there are still all too many who think cigarettes are cool. They're not – they're killers. Use your head and don't start, or if you have, get help in giving up. There are various methods of managing withdrawal, and there's counselling and support. You'll be healthier, look better and have a lot more money.

Soaps

Soaps are fun to watch and provide a relaxing hour or two after a busy day. They're largely fantasy though, so don't take them too seriously. The same with reality shows – fun to see how people react and get on together, but remember they're in a forced environment and they too are performing for the cameras. They'd probably be quite different if you met them in ordinary life.

Spots   *see Acne*

Stress

see also Depression, Fear, Panic

Most of us feel stressed out at some time or other. Stress can have many different causes, from family problems and relationship difficulties to exam pressure or bereavement. Even happy occasions like parties or holidays can create a degree of stress. Some stress is inevitable, but too much can cause real problems. If things are getting on top of you and causing a high level of stress, you may feel tired, run down, tearful, moody, depressed or even unusually aggressive. You may feel tension in the muscles of your neck, shoulders and back and you may have difficulty sleeping. Some people believe that alcohol, smoking or drugs can help relax someone who is tense, but this is an illusion. These substances may help short-term, but will cause more stress and damage our bodies in the long run.

Get advice from your doctor. Talk to a teacher or tutor if work is bothering you. Try some outdoor activity or working-out at a gym. Don't be too shy to ask for prayer from your church or Christian youth group.

Suffering

One of the most common questions asked of Christians is why God allows suffering, especially when it happens to innocent people, i.e. children, or famine victims, or war casualties, or the elderly.

It's a hard one to answer and often we can't. We know,

though, that God's heart breaks over the suffering that he sees in his children. He gave us the gift of free will and the responsibility of choice. All of us can either accept God into our lives or reject him. Sadly, the majority still refuse to accept him. We may get angry with God over the suffering we see in the world, but if we're honest, isn't it often the result of man's greed, hatred and the turning away from God's laws?

(Read 1 Peter 3:8-22.)

Tt

Teachers
see also School

A great deal of our time in teenage years is spent in close proximity to teachers, whether we like it or not. You may love or loathe your teacher. If you are fortunate enough to have a real rapport with your teacher, he or she can be a real inspiration and help in achieving your chosen goals. There may be a few sadistic bullies among teachers, though maybe not as many as you would like to think. A teacher can be a good confidante, example and encourager, as well as actually instructing you. Remember, though, that they're not supermen and women! They're only human and may have bad days too.

Text-Messaging

You may think that text-message-speak was invented by the current generation of mobile phone users. You'd be wrong. The message below and others like it was around at least fifty years ago, maybe more; 'yy u r, yy u b, I c u r yy 4 me.' Lol!

Thank you

Thank you is not too difficult to say, but it is something often overlooked. These two small words can make a lot of difference. Saying thanks for a present or card, help or advice, a message or a prayer, friendly support, or even thanking a parent or teacher who's been there for you, not only encourages the giver but makes you feel good too. Most of all, God deserves our thanks for his unconditional love. (Read Luke 17:11-19.)

Travel

They say that travel broadens the mind. It also lightens the pocket and causes many a grey hair and wrinkle to the parents, especially if the traveller has set off with not much more than a backpack, high hopes, and no forwarding address. It's some comfort that Internet cafes have sprung up almost everywhere making email links possible, and that mobile phones can provide instant contact. (Worrying though if you can't get a signal, and find out charges for where you're going – many a parent has been unpleasantly surprised by gigantic bills!)

Some people are born travellers and some like to stay put. The fortunate ones get to go on holidays abroad, usually a vast improvement on family holidays in general. School exchanges are an excellent way of sampling another way of life, a different (preferably warmer) climate, unusual food, learning another language and gaining confidence along the way. You'll be free of parental interference too, though if you're with a family, your host parents will take on that responsibility.

There are other ways of seeing the world too, notably the summer projects and missions organised by various Christian organisations, when a group or team of young people participate in helping Third World or European countries in a variety of 'hands on' ways. You will probably have to be very fit, a committed Christian, and you will have to be prepared to work hard and raise your own funds for the trip, but this kind of adventure can be most fulfilling, enriching and rewarding, and will probably alter your perspective on life for good.

Uu

UFOs

Stories abound about Unidentified Flying Objects, and all kinds of other extra-terrestrial phenomena, fuelled by a flood of books, videos and movies. We do not know if there is life beyond our galaxy, though wonders of new discovery daily unfold before our eyes through science, technology, space exploration and from the wonders of the natural world. The Bible speaks of the planets and the stars, but it does not say whether life exists on them. Whether or not, it is all under the control and Lordship of our creator God.

Ugly

Beauty is supposed to be in the eye of the beholder, and maybe ugliness is too. Most teenage girls, however much of a babe they might seem to others, are prone to peering into mirrors and uttering cries of despair because they do not seem to measure up to some pop idol.

A spot or two, or a misjudged hair colour, even the inherited shape of a nose, can convince you you're the most unattractive object ever!

Don't you believe it! You are lovely in God's sight and very probably lovely in the sight of others too.

Valentines

Hearts beat faster as Valentine's Day comes round again. How many pink or red or blue, heart-shaped or frilly, funny or romantic (or even rude) cards will plop through your letter box or pop up on your screen this year? Will you know who they're from or will you be left guessing and tantalised? What happens (horrors!) if no one sends you a Valentine? Or what if you find out that the one you've been puzzling over turns out to be only from your mum?

Then there's the problem of deciding who you're going to send one to (or more than one), the choice of card, the wording of the cryptic message, and the delicious anticipation of wondering whether the recipient will guess it's from you. Better give him a clue, just in case.

Vegetarianism *see also Cooking, Diets, Food*

Many people are opting for vegetarianism today, especially younger people. Vegetarians do not eat red meat in any form, though some may eat a little chicken or fish. Vegans have much stricter rules, omitting even fish, eggs and dairy products.

You may choose to be vegetarian for reasons of conscience, i.e. as a protest against meat raised in an intensive, factory-type environment. You may think a meat-free diet is healthier, or you may simply dislike meat and meat products. The Bible rules allow for meat eating but don't insist upon it. It's a personal choice.

If you've decided on vegetarianism, make sure you have alternative proteins and vitamins in your diet. Cheese, wholegrain cereals, pasta, pulses, soya products, fruits and vegetables will provide what is necessary for proper nutrition and good health.

Verbal Abuse *see also Bullying*

No one, but no one, should feel they have to put up with verbal abuse. It can be one of the most hurtful of things, and is a very unpleasant aspect of bullying. People who are different in some way that makes them stand out from the crowd are often targets for verbal abuse. It's cowardly and it's cheap.

Christians often come in for their share. If possible, draw strength from other Christians. We're told to pray for those who treat us badly. If you're vulnerable and you're really getting upset by verbal abuse, something should be done. Tell a teacher, a tutor or a parent. This kind of nastiness should be firmly nipped in the bud.

Voice

It's a shock to hear your voice on tape for the first time. Can those squeaky, giggly, alien-sounding tones really be the way you speak? Is that what your boyfriend hears every time he rings your mobile number?

Don't be too quick to rush out and book elocution lessons. There's nothing wrong with your voice and there's nothing wrong with a regional accent. Be proud of your background. Don't try to talk posh. It'll sound dafter than ever and you'll only get stressed out trying to keep it up.

Ww

War

There have always been wars, and always will be. In the pages of Scripture and down throughout history, war has followed war. There are resources enough for everyone on the earth, but something in the heart of humankind pushes us to fight our fellows time and again.

Acts of terrorism bring a new and horrifying dimension to our society and new arguments for and against war reach fever pitch. We seem ever more far away from reaching a state of peace on earth.

Most people don't want war but feel powerless in the face of the activated war machine. We may launch protests and campaign for the end of wars, but real change only comes when the hearts of individuals are transformed by knowing the Lord Jesus Christ. Only in his kingdom will war finally come to an end. Each person committing their life to God will take a step towards the coming of peace.

Why?

see Questions

Work

see also Careers

Unless you're the least motivated person on earth, everyone enjoys work of some kind or other. It may be physical, pottering in the kitchen or taking a car engine to pieces. Or it may be mental work, or something involving technology – planning a website or writing a best seller. School and college work loom large all through your teen years, and you will probably have work experience or Saturday and holiday jobs to earn some cash for yourself. Sooner or later, you'll be projected into the big world where everyone works for real to keep a roof over their head and food on the table. Now is the time to prepare for that, aiming for the best qualifications so that you ultimately find and enjoy the work you're best suited for.

Worries

see Fear, Panic

Worship

Worship is an essential part of knowing God, who created us just for that purpose. When we have a relationship with Jesus Christ, it is natural to want to worship him for what he has done and above all, for who and what he is. We can worship God in many ways; in prayer, singing, clapping, dancing, with instruments or by using our creative gifts, with others or quietly on our own.

Worship focuses upon God and brings a sense of his presence in a way that perhaps nothing else can. Worship is an important part of their experience for most Christian young people. They are usually less inhibited than older people and less bound by tradition. Worshipping God, alone or with others, is one of the most precious and meaningful privileges afforded to us. (Read Psalm 47.)

Wrinklies

They're old (and they act like it), well past it, out of touch, dated and inhibited. They don't like your music, they struggle over the internet, they disapprove of late nights, enthusiasm, cool gear, some of your friends and most of your culture.

They're also experienced, long-suffering, not as daft as you may think (some are even on Facebook!) hard-working and caring. They know a thing or two. (Well, they brought you up, didn't they?)

X – the Unknown Quantity

see also Occult

There's a great deal of interest these days in the supernatural and the unexplained. It's probably because we've all grown weary of the materialistic and are looking for a spiritual dimension in this post-modern age.

Don't be fooled! The only genuine supernatural experience is the one we enter into by becoming reconciled to God through his Son.

Youth Groups

A good Christian Youth Group is perhaps the best asset a young believer can have. The group will supply strength, friendship, encouragement and support. A wise leader will gain the confidence of the individual members, give an ear to listen, and advice and prayer if needed. A group provides much-needed discussion, humour and fun. You'll go on holidays and outings, to conferences and houseparties together. If one falters, there'll be others who can be strong for them.

If you're not fortunate enough to have a group nearby, find another Christian so that you can support one another as prayer partners. There are plenty of good Christian groups on the internet too.

Zits

see Acne

Some contact addresses, phone numbers and websites

AIDS
National Aids helpline: (0800) 567123
www.thewellproject.org

Alcohol Abuse
Alcoholics Anonymous (AA),
London helpline: (0171) 352 3001.
Head Office, PO Box 1,
Stonebow House, York YOI 7NJ.
(01904) 644026

Alcohol Action Wales, 8th Floor,
Brunel House, 2 Fitzlan Rd,
Cardiff CF2 1EB
www.alcoholics-anonymous.org

Childline
(0800)1111. Freepost 1111,
London N1 ORR

NSPCC Childline: (0800) 800500
www.ChildLine.co.uk

Christian Holidays and Mission Projects
Scripture Union:
207 – 209 Queensway, Bletchley,
Milton Keynes MK2 2EB.
Tel: (01908) 856000.
Fax: (01908) 856111
www.scriptureunion.org.uk

Crusaders (Crusoe):
2, Romeland Hill, St. Albans, Herts
AL3 4ET

World Horizons, North Dock Centre,
Llanelli Dyfed.
www.worldhorizons.co.uk

Drug Abuse   Lifeline: (90161) 8392054

Re-Solv (Society for Prevention of
Solvent and Volatile Substance Abuse):
30a High St, Stone, Staffs ST15 8AW
www.drugfree.org

Eating Disorders   Youth Helpline: (01603) 765050
Mon – Fri, 4 – 6 pm

The Eating Disorder Association:
First Floor, Wensum House,
103 Prince of Wales Rd, Norwich,
Norfolk NR1 1DW. (01603) 621414

The Anorexia and Bulimia Nervosa
Association, Tottenham Women and
Health Centre Annexe, Tottenham,
London N15 4RK
www.nationaleatingdisorders.org

Giving up Smoking	Smoker's Quitline: Wales: (01222) 0641888 London: (0171) 4873000
	ASH (Action for Smoking and Health), 5-11 Mortimer Street, London W1A 4QW www.nhs.uk/gosmokefree
Pregnancy Advice	Care Centre Network: CARE (0800) 0282228 www.pregnancy.org.uk www.christiananswers.net/pregnancy

Eleanor Watkins can be contacted through the publisher's address at the front of the book. She can also be found on Facebook!